the Grand Canyon

·········· FROM RIM TO RIVER ··········

RIO NUEVO PUBLISHERS
TUCSON, ARIZONA

contents

Leave it as it is. You cannot improve on it.
The ages have been at work on it, and man can only
mar it. What you can do is to keep it for your children,
your children's children, and for all who come after
you, as one of the great sights which every American
if he can travel at all should see.

— PRESIDENT THEODORE ROOSEVELT,
MAY 6, 1903, FROM HIS SPEECH AT THE SOUTH RIM

Introduction 1

ABOVE: Great blue herons wade in the Colorado River, dining on fish as well as other small animals.

RIGHT: The Colorado River flows through Marble Canyon.

Many say the Grand Canyon is the planet's history book—two billion years inscribed on the multicolored strata of its cliffs and canyons. Ignored by Europeans and Americans for centuries, it is now one of the most visited natural wonders. This World Heritage Site holds an array of geological, historical, and biological treasures that is unmatched at any other place. The elements, plants and animals, and humans have all made their mark on the canyon in significant ways. They are all part of this well-preserved history book, which also offers one of the most stunning visual spectacles on earth.

The experts say that it takes months, years, or even a lifetime to truly get to know the canyon. Shadows and light constantly ebb and flow, and the changing seasons bring flashes of lightning, shimmering rainbows, and blankets of snow. The entire color spectrum can be found here. We are fortunate that so many photographers have fallen in love with the canyon and are willing to share their art with us on these pages.

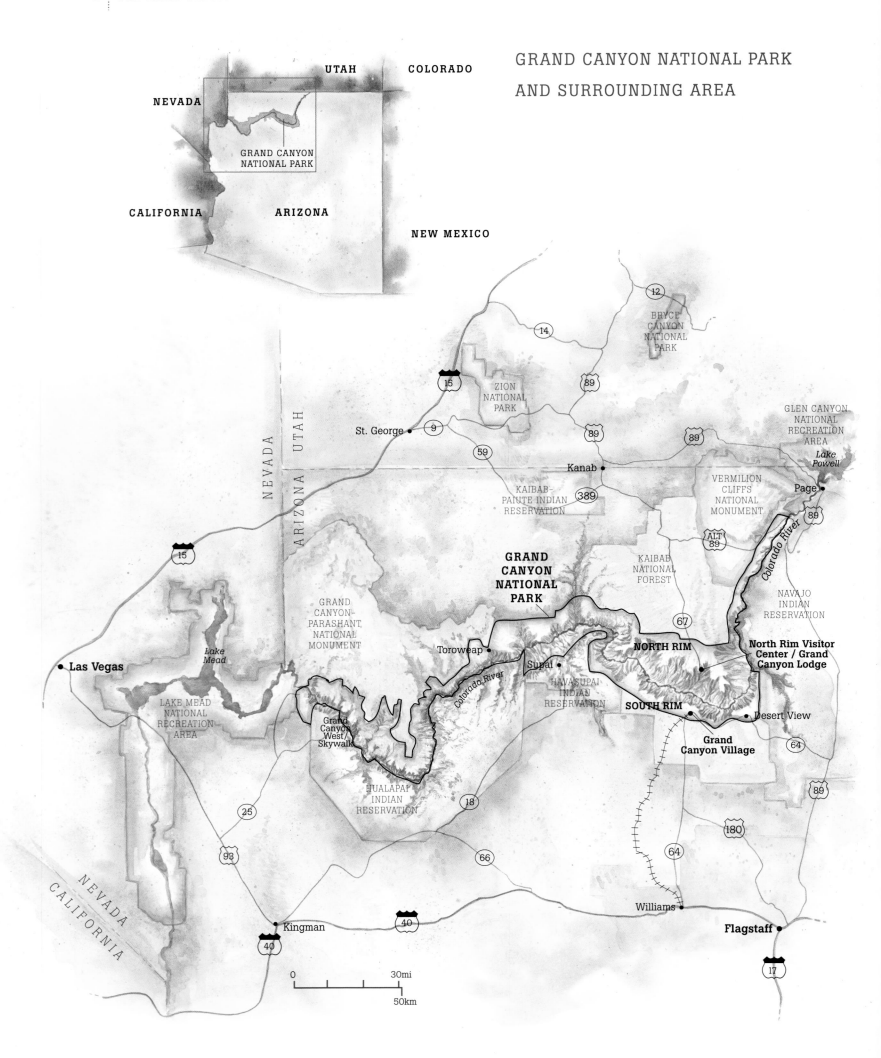

GRAND CANYON NATIONAL PARK
AND SURROUNDING AREA

UTAH   COLORADO

NEVADA

GRAND CANYON
NATIONAL PARK

CALIFORNIA   ARIZONA

NEW MEXICO

BRYCE
CANYON
NATIONAL
PARK

ZION
NATIONAL
PARK

GLEN CANYON
NATIONAL
RECREATION
AREA

*Lake
Powell*

St. George

Kanab

Page

KAIBAB-
PAIUTE INDIAN
RESERVATION

VERMILION
CLIFFS
NATIONAL
MONUMENT

NEVADA

ARIZONA
UTAH

Colorado River

KAIBAB
NATIONAL
FOREST

NAVAJO
INDIAN
RESERVATION

GRAND
CANYON
NATIONAL
PARK

GRAND
CANYON-
PARASHANT
NATIONAL
MONUMENT

*Lake
Mead*

Las Vegas

Toroweap

Supai

Colorado River

NORTH RIM

**North Rim Visitor
Center / Grand
Canyon Lodge**

HAVASUPAI
INDIAN
RESERVATION

SOUTH RIM

Desert View

LAKE MEAD
NATIONAL
RECREATION
AREA

Grand
Canyon
West /
Skywalk

**Grand
Canyon Village**

HUALAPAI
INDIAN
RESERVATION

NEVADA

CALIFORNIA

Kingman

Williams

Flagstaff

0   30mi

50km

The Grand Canyon was formed by an incredibly long sequence of weathering, erosion, sedimentation, volcanism, faulting, and uplifting. Weathering is the decomposition of rocks, soils, and minerals by heat, air, water, and pressure. Erosion is similar but involves the wearing away of rocks by the movement of wind, water, and the particles they carry with them. These particles eventually settle on the earth's surface or on the bottom of lakes and oceans. There they harden into flat-layered sedimentary rock formations.

A larger global process called *plate tectonics* causes volcanoes and faults. According to plate tectonics theory, the earth's hard crust broke into pieces called *tectonic plates*, which continue to bump into each other or pull away, causing earthquakes, volcanic activity, and uplifts where the plates overlap.

Volcanism occurs when hot liquid magma, ash, and gases from deep inside the earth burst through openings in the earth's crust. The magma becomes molten lava, which cools and hardens into igneous rock.

Faults occur when pressure cracks the earth's crust into pieces that move in separate directions. Uplift raises a block of rock and soil upward

HOW THE GRAND CANYON WAS FORMED

Brightly colored collared lizards can be found basking on rocks at lower elevations in the canyon.

several thousand feet but leaves it as flat as the area around it, forming a plateau.

Eons of pushing up, wearing down, and washing away created the canyon we see today. The hardness and resistance of each type of rock determines what remains and what crumbles away.

The Vishnu Schist at the bottom was formed as sediment, lava, and ash collided with the continent about 1.7 billion years ago. Once the collision ceased, slow uplift over hundreds of millions of years, with concurrent erosion on the surface, exposed the rocks.

GEOLOGY OF THE GRAND CANYON

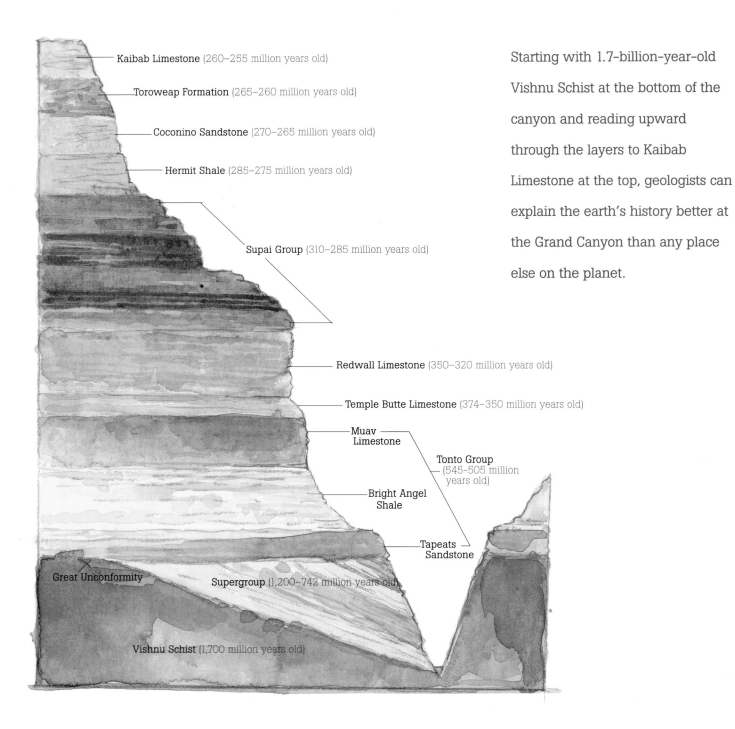

Kaibab Limestone (260–255 million years old)

Toroweap Formation (265–260 million years old)

Coconino Sandstone (270–265 million years old)

Hermit Shale (285–275 million years old)

Supai Group (310–285 million years old)

Redwall Limestone (350–320 million years old)

Temple Butte Limestone (374–350 million years old)

Muav Limestone

Tonto Group (545–505 million years old)

Bright Angel Shale

Tapeats Sandstone

Great Unconformity

Supergroup (1,200–742 million years old)

Vishnu Schist (1,700 million years old)

Starting with 1.7-billion-year-old Vishnu Schist at the bottom of the canyon and reading upward through the layers to Kaibab Limestone at the top, geologists can explain the earth's history better at the Grand Canyon than any place else on the planet.

After the period of erosion, more than 10,000 feet of sediment were deposited on sea floors in the area. About 800 million years ago, massive faulting tilted up a series of mountains.

About 16 million years ago, pressure under the earth's crust raised the Colorado Plateau several thousand feet above sea level. Finally, six million years ago the Colorado River began cutting through the plateau and eventually reached the earliest rocks thousands of feet below the surface. It was not the water that did the cutting, however, but the constant grinding of pebbles, rocks, and even boulders that rumble through the canyon and give the Colorado River its roar.

Geological forces continue to sculpt the Grand Canyon. The river works at the bottom of the canyon, while weathering and erosion continue to carve its walls.

Mount Hayden is framed by a natural limestone window on the North Rim.

ELEVATION, CLIMATE, AND BIODIVERSITY

The Grand Canyon's range of elevations, climates, and geological features allows a great biodiversity of plant and animal species to thrive. Biotic communities span from desertscrub at the bottom of the canyon to spruce-fir forest on the North Rim. 1,800 plant, 355 bird, 89 mammal, 47 reptile, 17 fish, and 19 amphibian species call the Grand Canyon home.

ANCIENT AND MODERN INDIANS

Four thousand years ago prehistoric hunters and gatherers now known as the Desert Culture wove small figures that looked like deer and mountain sheep out of split willow twigs. They pierced them with spear-like sticks as a ritual to ensure good hunting. These artifacts have been found in the recesses of the inner Grand Canyon.

Around AD 1 these same ancestors of the modern Pueblo and Hopi tribes moved to the Four Corners area (where Arizona, Utah, Colorado, and New Mexico meet) and began farming. They wove rabbit-fur blankets and lived in caves or rock shelters. They are known as the "Basketmakers" because of the numerous baskets associated with their sites.

Around AD 500 the Basketmakers added beans and cotton to their crops. They built circular pit houses, created clay pottery, and expanded their territory almost back to the Grand Canyon. The additional food supplies freed up time to produce ceramic art, decorated pottery, and woven cotton cloth.

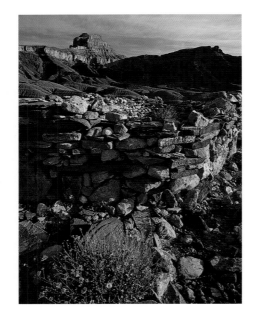

ABOVE: Brittlebush grows beside an Ancestral Puebloan ruin.

RIGHT: A rainbow, seen from Bright Angel Point on the North Rim, curves over the canyon. At the end of the Bright Angel Point peninsula, you might hear Roaring Springs down below, the canyon's source for drinking water.

People of the Pueblo I culture, named for their apartment-style dwellings, began to explore and live seasonally in the east end of the canyon around AD 700. They lived along the rim but not in the canyon. By AD 1000, a large influx of Pueblo II peoples, known for their large stone masonry communal pueblos such as those found at Mesa Verde, occupied hundreds of sites on both rims and in recesses in the canyon itself.

Also at that time the Southern Paiutes, a non-Pueblo people, migrated from Utah to the north rim of the Grand Canyon, and the Cohoninas moved in from west-central Arizona. Probably because of drought, the Puebloans and Cohoninas abandoned the canyon around AD 1200.

The Cerbat Indians, ancestors of the modern Havasupais and Hualapais (the Pai people) then occupied the south banks of the Colorado all through the canyon to the Little Colorado River on the eastern edge. The Paiutes moved in along the north rim, sometimes occupying abandoned Pueblo ruins. Both Pai and Paiute people maintained friendly trade relations with the Pueblos and present-day Hopis.

In 1540, conquistador Francisco Vásquez de Coronado explored the West, claiming lands for King Charles V and searching for the fabled Seven Cities of Gold. Coronado sent Captain Garcia López de Cárdenas to the Grand Canyon's South Rim. Three of his soldiers hiked one-third of the way down and said that a rock that looked as tall as a man from the rim was actually "bigger than the great tower of Seville."

It is old, this Grand Canyon, and yet so new it seems almost to smell of paint—red paint, pink, and scarlet.

—JOAQUIN MILLER, AMERICAN POET, 1901

SPANISH EXPLORATION

In 1776, centuries after Coronado's failed mission, Father Francisco Garcés reached the Grand Canyon from the west and encountered the Havasupais in Havasu Canyon. The following year, seeking to link the New Mexico and California missions, fathers Francisco Dominguez and Silvestre Escalante traveled along the North Rim of the Grand Canyon. They chiseled steps into the sandstone walls of Glen Canyon (later called El Vado de los Padres, meaning "the crossing of the fathers") to cross the Colorado River. The Grand Canyon was just a travel obstruction for the Spaniards, and they never visited again. Europeans then avoided the canyon and its inhabitants for more than fifty years.

ABOVE: Major John Wesley Powell led the first known expedition down the Colorado River through the Grand Canyon in 1869. His descriptive popular magazine articles about his river expeditions brought widespread attention to the canyon.

RIGHT: Deer Creek tumbles over Tapeats Sandstone in Deer Creek Gorge.

U.S. EXPLORATION

In 1857, the U.S. Army sent Lieutenant Joseph Christmas Ives and a small crew up the Colorado River in a small paddle-wheeled steamboat. The expedition steamed up the Colorado to the rapids at Black Canyon (near where Hoover Dam is today) then continued on foot along the South Rim. In his report, Ives said, "Ours has been the first, and doubtless will be the last party of whites to visit this profitless locality. It seems intended by nature that the Colorado River along the greater part of its lonely and majestic way, shall be forever unvisited and undisturbed."

Major John Wesley Powell, who had lost his right arm in the Civil War, led the first known river trip through the Grand Canyon. On May 24, 1869, ten men in four boats started at Green River City, Wyoming, and followed the Green River until it merged with the Colorado River. In 1874, Powell's *Scribner's Monthly* articles about his two canyon expeditions, illustrated with engravings drawn from Jack Hillers' photographs, brought national attention to the canyon's majestic beauty.

A NATIONAL PARK IS CREATED

In 1886, Indiana Senator (later President) Benjamin Harrison began the campaign to make the Grand Canyon a national park. Politics and private interests delayed the process, but the area was designated a national forest in 1893. In spite of this protection, damages and unlawful land seizures occurred.

President Theodore Roosevelt proclaimed the Grand Canyon a national monument in 1908, without the consent of Congress, to provide more protection for the canyon. For the next ten years various Grand Canyon National Park bills were fought out between private interests and the government. Finally, Congress voted on a compromise and President Woodrow Wilson signed the bill creating Grand Canyon National Park in 1919. During the Great Depression (1929–1941) a federal program called the Civilian Conservation Corps built trails, picnic shelters, campgrounds, and telephone lines in the canyon.

President Theodore Roosevelt rides a mule on a canyon trail.

But the colors, the living, rejoicing colors, chanting morning and evening in chorus to heaven! Whose brush or pencil, however lovingly inspired, can give us these? And if paint is of no effect, what hope lies there in pen-work? Only this: some may be incited by it to go and see for themselves.

—JOHN MUIR,
NATURALIST,
THE GRAND CANYON OF THE COLORADO, 1902

South Rim

2

ABOVE: A California condor soars above the canyon.

RIGHT: Clearing winter storm over Isis Temple, from Hopi Point.

Most of the five million people who visit the Grand Canyon each year see it from the South Rim. The South Rim is the most easily accessible and developed part of the park. This is where the crowds come to gaze in awe on the great chasm that nature has created and continues to create. Ten miles across the canyon, the higher and more remote North Rim rises.

At an average elevation of 7,000 feet, the South Rim experiences the full range of seasons. Summer temperatures top out in the 80s (degrees F). July, August, and early September bring monsoonal thunderstorms, torrential rains, and flash floods. Winter temperatures dip into the teens but rise to the 40s (degrees F) due to sunny days. However, snow and ice are not uncommon, and the average annual snowfall is 50–100+ inches on the rim, occasionally blanketing the canyon all the way down to the river below.

The South Rim is home to pinyon-juniper woodland and ponderosa pine forest communities, with species such as gray fox, mule deer, bighorn sheep, and Abert squirrels.

Grand Canyon Village is the center of activity on the South Rim. The Historic District was built by the Santa Fe Railroad during the first half of the twentieth century. Lookout Studio, a photography studio designed by architect Mary Colter, blends into the canyon wall. It now serves visitors as a gift shop and observation station. Railroad worker Bill Kent proposed to "Harvey Girl" waitress Betty Priest under the Lookout Studio, but he always joked that *she* asked *him,* and threatened to push him over the edge if he didn't say yes!

This composite image of the canyon near Mather Point shows an August

sunrise on the left, and a June sunset on the right.

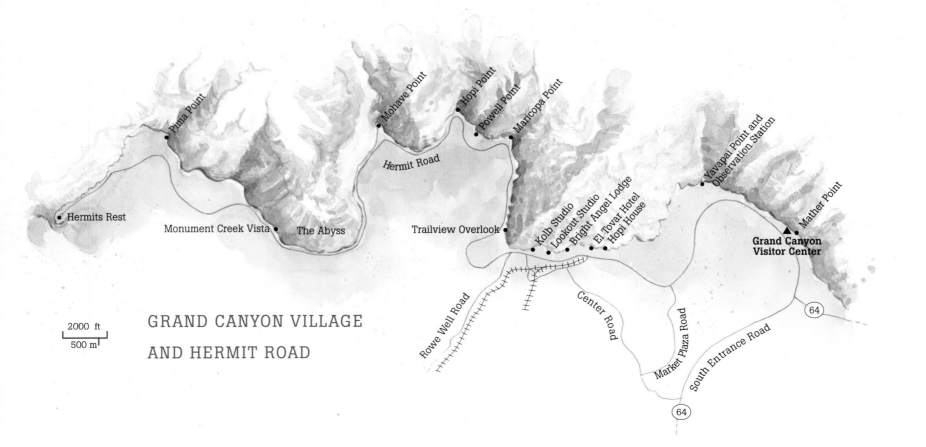

Hermits Rest

Pima Point

Monument Creek Vista

The Abyss

Hermit Road

Mohave Point

Hopi Point

Powell Point

Maricopa Point

Trailview Overlook

Kolb Studio

Lookout Studio

Bright Angel Lodge

El Tovar Hotel

Hopi House

Vavapai Point and
Observation Station

Mather Point

**Grand Canyon
Visitor Center**

Rowe Well Road

Center Road

Market Plaza Road

South Entrance Road

64

64

2000 ft
500 m

GRAND CANYON VILLAGE
AND HERMIT ROAD

The map at left shows Grand Canyon Village and the overlooks along Hermit Road. Scenic Hermit Road winds along the rim for seven miles from Grand Canyon Village west to Hermits Rest. Private vehicles are allowed on this road only during winter months. During the rest of the year visitors may follow this route by free shuttle bus, foot, bicycle, or commercial bus.

Mather Point (7,120 feet), adjacent to the park's entrance, is a crowded but spectacular viewpoint. This overlook was named for Stephen Mather, the first director of the National Park Service.

Yavapai Point (7,040 feet), shown here at sunset, overlooks Comanche Point (the highest knob on the horizon), Desert Palisades, and Vishnu Temple (glowing red in the waning light).

The first view of the Canyon springs upon the visitor with the leap of a panther, and suggesting a deserted world, yawns at his feet before he is aware that he is within miles of it. It overwhelms him by its suddenness, and renders him speechless with its grandeur and magnificence.

—GEORGE WHARTON JAMES,
IN AND OUT OF THE GRAND CANYON,
1900

Pennsylvanian Ellsworth Kolb arrived at the Grand Canyon in 1901 and persauded his brother Emery to join him the following year. They captured stunning photographs of the Grand Canyon and toured the East showing the movies taken on their boat trips through the canyon in the early 1900s. Emery Kolb (shown at left hanging from a rock with his camera) ran the film several times a day for more than sixty years, making it the longest-running film in history. The brothers built a studio perched on the lip of the canyon next to Bright Angel Trail, and photographed the tourists who rode mules into the canyon.

Ours has been the first, and will doubtless be the last party of whites to visit this profitless locality... It seems intended by nature that the Colorado, along the greater part of its lonely and majestic way, shall be forever unvisited and undisturbed.

—Lieutenant Joseph Christmas Ives, 1861

A Utah juniper soaks up a little sunlight after a winter storm at Maricopa Point (6,995 feet). This view looks out to the North Rim across the canyon.

Powell Point (7,040 feet) is named for John Wesley Powell, who led the first known expedition down the Colorado River through the Grand Canyon in 1869. Powell Memorial honors his achievements. In this photo taken at the memorial, smoke rises in the distance from a lightning fire.

The swift-rushing river is dashing and flashing its way to the sea, but it is so far off that you grasp neither its form nor its fury.

—John C. Van Dyke
Art critic and nature writer

LEFT: The sun lights up Zoroaster Temple and the canyon below Hopi Point (6,800 feet). Hopi Point juts out farther into the canyon than any other overlook on the South Rim, and its wide vistas offer stunning views of sunrise and sunset.

BELOW AND RIGHT: Mohave Point (6,995 feet) is another popular sunrise and sunset viewpoint. A red promontory called the Alligator, shown at right, stretches out into the canyon.

Most Grand Canyon viewpoints jut out into the canyon, but the Abyss offers a staggering, almost vertical view down into the Monument Creek drainage area. The Great Mohave Wall towers over the inner canyon, and Isis Temple is visible in the distance.

On a quiet day at Pima Point (6,798 feet), you might be able to hear the roar of Granite Falls, one of the largest rapids in the canyon. Pima Point's panorama stretches from Powell Plateau in the west to Cape Royal in the east. The Greenway Trail, also known as the Rim Trail, continues from here to Hermits Rest.

The end of Hermit Road brings you to Hermits Rest at 6,650 feet elevation. Hermits Rest offers a good view of Dripping Springs Canyon, where "The Hermit," Louis Boucher, lived around the turn of the twentieth century. Mary Colter designed Hermits Rest in 1914 in the style of an old miner's cabin. She disliked El Tovar Hotel's Swiss chalet style and preferred to copy Arizona's ancient dwellings. Hermits Rest is a good example of this, with its arch of uneven stones and broken mission bell. When someone asked her, "Why don't you clean up this place?" she replied, "You can't imagine what it cost to make it look this old."

The photo at right shows a river-to-rim view of the Hermits Rest area. The rock face displays the full spectrum of Grand Canyon rock layers, from Vishnu Schist at the bottom to Kaibab Limestone at the top.

This map illustrates the overlooks along Desert View Drive, a scenic route that follows the rim for twenty-five miles east from Grand Canyon Village to the Desert View Watchtower. Private vehicles are permitted year-round.

DESERT VIEW DRIVE

Desert bighorn sheep can be found in desertscrub and pinyon-juniper plant communities. They are known for navigating the canyon's steep cliffs and rough terrain with ease. A male's horns can weigh up to thirty pounds.

Yaki Point (7,262 feet) can be reached by the Kaibab Trail Route Shuttle, by tour bus, or by walking the Rim Trail. Yaki Point is a quiet place to view sunrise or sunset, with sweeping views to the east and west. Vishnu Temple and Wotan's Throne are across the canyon, and Pattie's Butte glows red in the sunlight below. The southwesterly slope of the Kaibab Plateau below Yaki Point causes South Rim rain to flow away from the canyon and North Rim rain to fall into the canyon, which causes more erosion and therefore continues to make the North Rim farther away from the river than the South Rim.

There is a certain malady, commonly
termed 'big head,' with which a large
number of otherwise healthy people are
afflicted. Prescription: Stand upon the brink
of the Grand Canyon, gaze down, and still
further down, into its awful depths, and
realize for the first time your own
utter insignificance.

—MARY E. HART, M.D., 1895

RIGHT: Rime ice coats a branch of Gambel oak at Yaki Point.

BELOW: Grandview Point (7,399 feet), one of the highest overlooks on the
South Rim and lush with ponderosa pines, offers panoramic views of the
canyon from east to west. The steep Grandview Trail begins here.

Moran Point (7,160 feet) is named after Thomas Moran, a landscape painter who fell in love with the Grand Canyon when he joined John Wesley Powell's overland survey in 1873. He returned to the canyon almost every year until his death in 1926. This view looks out over layered Paleozoic sedimentary rocks that make up most of the canyon's depth.

This composite image of the panorama from Moran Point includes Ansel Adams's late-afternoon view of the Grand Canyon from 1941. Adams was employed by the U.S. Department of the Interior from 1941 to 1942 to photograph national parks in the West, including the Grand Canyon.

LEFT: The California condor is the largest bird in North America, with a wingspan of ten feet, and is also one of the rarest birds in the world. It was brought to the brink of extinction by the early twentieth century, in large part due to lead poisoning by ingestion of lead ammunition in the carcasses these birds feed on. Later in the century the recovery effort began, which now has resulted in condors flying freely in California, Utah, and Arizona skies, including over the Grand Canyon.

BELOW: From Lipan Point (7,360 feet), you can look down onto Unkar Delta, a winding curve of the Colorado River, and Unkar Creek Rapid. Ancestral Puebloan people once made their winter home here, and it is now an active archeological site.

ABOVE: Sunset at Navajo Point (7,460 feet) swathes the canyon in red and orange.

LEFT: Feisty, dark-blue Steller's jays can often be seen trying to filch some crumbs from picnic tables and campsites.

The widely distributed common raven skillfully soars above the canyon.

Mountain lions inhabit the canyons and forests of the Grand Canyon and are the region's only remaining large predator. This shy cat is rarely seen.

Looking north from Desert View (7,438 feet): the Colorado River can be seen rushing below the Marble Platform. Desert View Watchtower, built in 1932, was designed by architect Mary Colter as a replica of an Ancestral Puebloan tower. Colter flew over several original prehistoric towers in a small plane before she visited them by car to sketch them and note building techniques. The seventy-five-foot-tall watchtower blends in with the landscape while providing the widest possible view of the canyon. Artwork by Hopi painter Fred Kabotie graces the inside.

LEFT: Kaibab squirrels are found only on the Kaibab Plateau in northern Arizona, on the North Rim. Known as the "Silver Ghosts of the North Rim," they bear the special designation of a National Natural Landmark. Their close relatives, the Abert squirrels, inhabit the South Rim. Kaibab and Abert squirrels make the best example of two closely related species separated by the canyon for many thousands of years. The Abert has a white belly and a grayish tail, while the Kaibab has a black belly and an almost white tail.

RIGHT: Sunrise from Toroweap Overlook.

North Rim

3

Only about ten percent of the Grand Canyon's tourists visit the North Rim, the forested and more remote side of the canyon. Though only ten miles across from the South Rim as the bird flies, it takes five hours to drive the 215 road miles from rim to rim. Hikers can also reach the North Rim by hiking 21 miles across the canyon from the South Rim. The North Rim is the place to get a quieter, off-the-beaten-path rim experience.

At an average elevation of 8,000 feet, the North Rim is higher and cooler than the South Rim. Summer temperatures top out in the 70s (degrees F), and winter highs stay closer to the freezing mark than at the South Rim. The North Rim is open to visitors only from mid-May through mid-October, when it is warmer and free of snow and ice.

The North Rim and the Kaibab plateau host ponderosa pine forest, spruce-fir forest (blue spruce, Engelmann spruce, Douglas fir, white fir, aspen, and mountain ash), and rare montane meadows and grassland communities. Mountain lions, Kaibab squirrels, and northern goshawks belong to these communities.

LEFT: Rocky Mountain elk, massive members of the deer family, can weigh up to a ton.

RIGHT: Autumn turns the canyon maple red on the west face of the Walhalla Plateau, north of Bright Angel Point. Brahma Temple rises up in the canyon beyond.

NORTH RIM OVERLOOKS AND ROADS

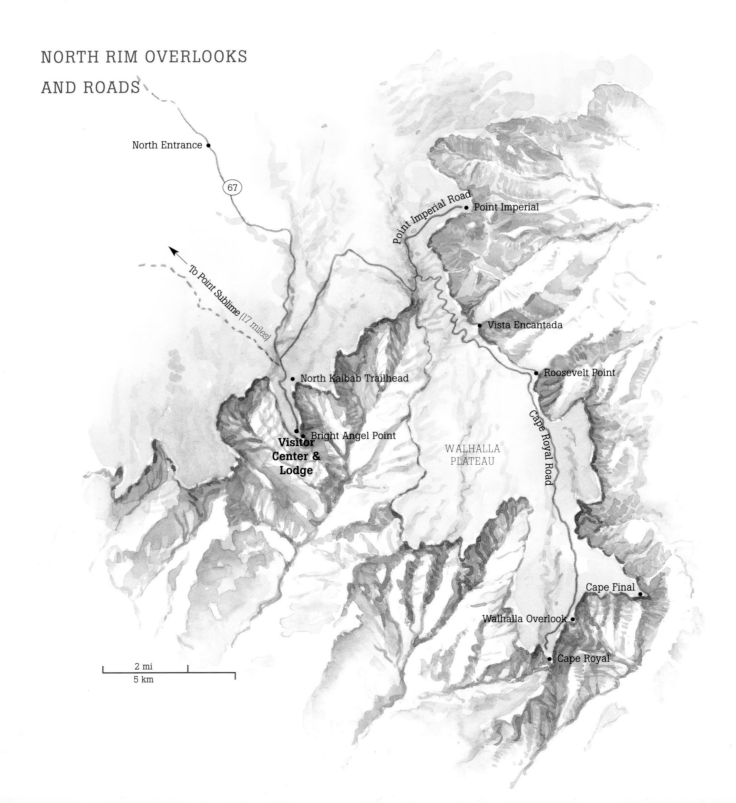

North Entrance

67

To Point Sublime (17 miles)

Point Imperial Road

Point Imperial

Vista Encantada

North Kaibab Trailhead

Roosevelt Point

Bright Angel Point

Visitor Center & Lodge

WALHALLA PLATEAU

Cape Royal Road

Cape Final

Walhalla Overlook

Cape Royal

2 mi
5 km

Point Imperial, at 8,803 feet, is the highest overlook at the Grand Canyon. Mount Hayden, shown here lit up by the sun, is a prominent Coconino sandstone formation that can be easily identified from Point Imperial.

Cape Royal's sweeping vistas to the east and west from 7,865 feet make it popular for sunrise and sunset viewing. Below, a sunrise illuminates Krishna Shrine, Vishnu Temple, and Freya Castle. Shown at right, the Colorado River makes a wide bend below Cedar Mountain in the distance.

A natural keyhole slot frames the view from Point Sublime.

Point Sublime (7,450 feet) can be found down a long dirt road west of the North Rim Visitor Center and is accessible only by 4-wheel-drive vehicles. Visitors to Point Sublime will discover a breathtaking and remote view extending east and west of the inner canyon. Shown at right, massive pillars of limestone stand tall.

RIGHT: The North Rim is home to quaking aspen, which get their name from leaves that flutter in even the softest breeze. Their bright green leaves turn yellow in the fall, giving a punch of color to the forest.

BELOW: Tuweep, a remote area on the northwest rim of the Grand Canyon, is challenging to reach, but visitors are rewarded at Toroweap Overlook (4,560 feet) with a dramatic view of a 3,000-foot vertical drop down to the Colorado River. This is one of the narrowest and deepest parts of the canyon, with less than a mile separating the North and South Rims as the crow flies. Ancient lava flows left basalt remnants on the rock below. Lava Falls Rapid is just downriver and can be easily seen and heard from the overlook. The Paiute name, "Toroweap," means "dry or barren valley." The Tuweep area, including Toroweap Overlook, is accessible from Fredonia or Colorado City, Arizona, or St. George, Utah, and is open year-round.

From terrace to terrace, climate to climate, down one creeps in sun and shade, through gorge and gully and grassy ravine, and, after a long scramble on foot, at last beneath the mighty cliffs one comes to the grand, roaring river.

—JOHN MUIR,
NATURALIST

Inner Canyon 4

ABOVE: A canyon wren sings atop a raft at the river.

RIGHT: Deer Creek Narrows.

The more adventurous visitor to the Grand Canyon can go beyond the sweeping vistas of the rims, into the depths of the inner canyon. Its rocks, waters, and caverns can be explored by foot, by mule, or by boat.

The inner canyon plunges as much as 6,000 feet below the rim, exposing layers of geologic strata from the basement Vishnu Schist to the top layer of Kaibab Limestone. Phantom Ranch, the stopover point for hikers and mule riders, sits nearly a mile below the rim. Architect Mary Colter designed this "deepest down ranch in the world" in 1922. It was built of local stone, but all other materials had to be brought down on mules.

Summer high temperatures at the river typically top 100 degrees F. In winter, cold air gets trapped in the canyon, leaving high temperatures only in the 40s and 50s (degrees F) and lows in 30s and 40s. Occasionally snowfall makes it all the way down to the river.

The inner canyon is home to a variety of biotic communities. The river's edge hosts riparian vegetation and sandy beaches, with red-spotted toads, great blue herons, beavers, coyotes, and ringtails. Just above the

river Mohave and Great Basin desertscrub communities thrive, with a wide variety of cacti and desert shrubs and trees, plus bats, rattlesnakes, lizards, and woodrats. Pinyon pine and juniper grow above the desertscrub up to 6,200 feet, and ponderosa pine grows above that up to 8,200 feet.

LEFT AND BELOW: The Colorado River winds 277 miles through Grand Canyon National Park from Lees Ferry to Lake Mead. The river runs 1,450 miles from its source in the Rocky Mountains of Colorado to the Gulf of California, and drops over 13,000 feet in elevation over its course. In the Grand Canyon, its average width is 300 feet, and its average depth is 40 feet.

ABOVE: Ringtails, adept climbers, are active at night in the inner canyon.

The three corridor trails—the North Kaibab, South Kaibab, and Bright Angel trails—all lead to Phantom Ranch at the bottom of the canyon; they are the only continuous trails that connect the North and South Rims. At right, a mule train makes its way up the South Kaibab Trail, traveling almost a vertical mile from the river back to the trailhead at the rim. All supplies used in the canyon are transported on the backs of mules.

BELOW: A hiker looks down over the Unkar rapid and delta. The Grand Canyon Supergroup rocks, shown here at the river, represent a significant portion of the canyon's geologic record, though only in isolated remnants.

Running water, the
smooth-edged winds, and
the silent frost have been the
only tools used here. The
hardness of the materials with
the softness of the tools but
emphasize the wonder of the
work. A sermon in patience
lies in the stone if we
shall read it right.

—JOHN C. VAN DYKE,
ART CRITIC AND NATURE WRITER

River runners camp on the sandy

beach of Whitmore Wash to explore

the area's geology. Black lava

cascades remain here as evidence

of ancient volcanic activity. The low

canyon walls make the trail up to

the rim the shortest river-to-rim

trail in the canyon.

The river became cleaner and quieter after it was dammed upstream, but there are still many rugged rapids to make the trip exciting. Below, a boater navigates Lava Falls, one of the last and most thrilling in the canyon. Most boating trips start from Lees Ferry and mix serenely calm waters with heart-pumping white-water rapids. To preserve its beauty, the National Park Service limits the number of people that can go through the canyon, but anyone who has run the rapids says it is worth the wait to experience the thrill and wonder of floating through the Grand Canyon.

RIGHT: Ancestral Puebloan people have left their mark on the canyon in the form of pictographs that still survive on the walls.

BELOW: Redwall Cavern, an impressively large cave, was carved from Redwall Limestone by the Colorado River.

BELOW: Muddy runoff flows down Marble Canyon's steep, narrow walls of Redwall Limestone. John Wesley Powell gave Marble Canyon its name because he thought the eroded sedimentary rocks resembled polished marble.

RIGHT: North Canyon's red Supai Group Sandstone has been carved into beguiling swirls by flooding water.

OPPOSITE: This beautiful stretch of the river near Nankoweap Canyon was once home to Ancestral Puebloan people, who farmed the fertile delta of Nankoweap Creek and built large granaries.

LEFT: Water rushes by maidenhair ferns at Havasu Creek.

BELOW: A tarantula crawls over a rock in Fossil Canyon.

LEFT: The Grand Canyon rattlesnake is not found anywhere else in the world. Its unique pale pink coloration differentiates it from the other five species of rattlesnakes that inhabit the canyon.

Often called "Shangri-la" or "Paradise," Havasu Canyon, located within the Havasupai Indian Reservation, is a large tributary on the south side of the Colorado River in the Grand Canyon, and can be accessed only by foot, mule or horse, or helicopter.

RIGHT: The vivid turquoise water of Havasu Creek flows through Havasu Canyon. Travertine, formed by calcium carbonate, coats the streambed, and the refraction of light gives the water its color.

OPPOSITE: Havasu Falls plunges 100 feet into blue-green pools separated by natural travertine dams.